SUGAR RA

Transcribed by BILL LaFLEUR &
HEMME LUTTJEBOER

Project Managers: AARON STANG &
SY FELDMAN

Book Art Layout: KEN REHM

CD Art Direction: LARRY FREEMANTLE

Photography: F. SCOTT SCHAFER

Illustration: DAN VICK

Thanks to CHIP QUIGLEY for his assistance

WARNER BROS. PUBLICATIONS - THE GLOBAL LEADER IN PRINT
USA: 15800 NW 48th Avenue, Miami, FL 33014

WARNER/CHAPPELL MUSIC

CANADA: 40 SHEPPARD AVE. WEST, SUITE 800
TORONTO, ONTARIO, M2N 6K9
SCANDINAVIA: P.O. BOX 533, VENDEVAGEN 85 B
S-182 15, DANDERYD, SWEDEN
AUSTRALIA: P.O. BOX 353
3 TALAVERA ROAD, NORTH RYDE N.S.W. 2113

Carisch
NUOVA CARISCH

ITALY: VIA CAMPANIA, 12
20098 S. GIULIANO MILANESE (MI)
ZONA INDUSTRIALE SESTO ULTERIANO
SPAIN: MAGALLANES, 25
28015 MADRID
FRANCE: 20, RUE DE LA VILLE-L'EVEQUE, 75008 PARIS

IMP
INTERNATIONAL MUSIC PUBLICATIONS LIMITED

ENGLAND: GRIFFIN HOUSE,
161 HAMMERSMITH ROAD, LONDON W6 8BS
GERMANY: MARSTALLSTR. 8, D-80539 MUNCHEN
DENMARK: DANMUSIK, VOGNMAGERGADE 7
DK 1120 KOBENHAVNK

CONTENTS

ABRACADABRA

Words and Music by
STEVE MILLER

All gtrs. tune down 1/2 step:

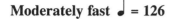

ⓖ = Eb   ③ = Gb

⑤ = Ab   ② = Bb

④ = Db   ① = Eb

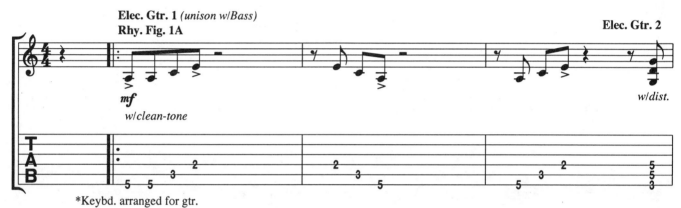

*Keybd. arranged for gtr.

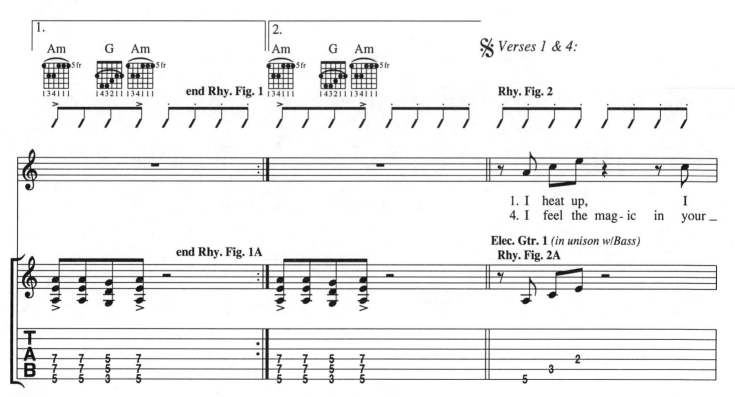

1. I heat up,   I
4. I feel the mag-ic in your_

Abracadabra – 7 – 1
0345B

end Rhy. Fig. 2

can't cool down. You've got me spin-ning 'round and 'round.
___ ca - ress. I feel ___ mag - ic when I touch your dress.

end Rhy. Fig. 2A

w/Rhy. Figs. 2 *(Keybd.)* & 2A *(Elec. Gtr. 1) simile*

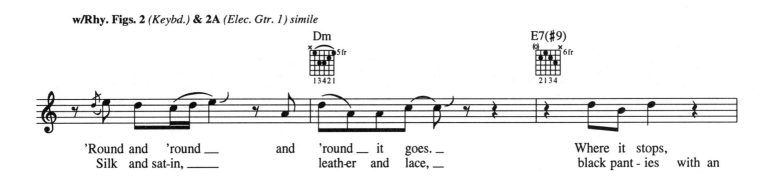

'Round and 'round ___ and 'round ___ it goes. ___ Where it stops,
Silk and sat-in, ___ leath-er and lace, ___ black pant - ies with an

Verses 2 & 5:

w/Rhy. Figs. 2 *(Keybd.)* & 2A *(Elec. Gtr. 1) 1 1/2 times, simile*

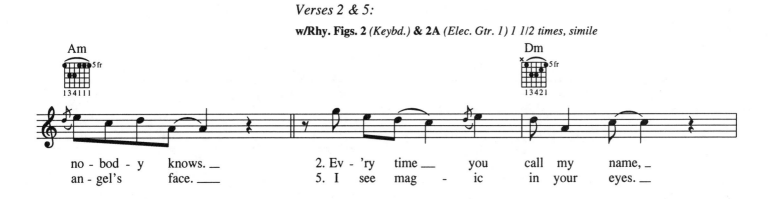

no - bod - y knows. ___ 2. Ev - 'ry time ___ you call my name, ___
an - gel's face. ___ 5. I see mag - ic in your eyes. ___

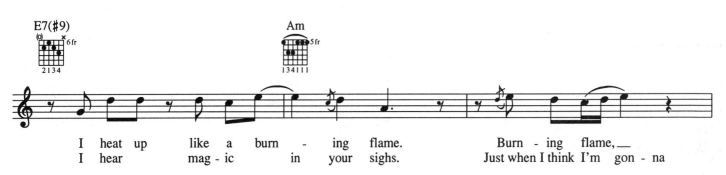

I heat up like a burn - ing flame. Burn - ing flame, ___
I hear mag - ic in your sighs. Just when I think I'm gon - na

8

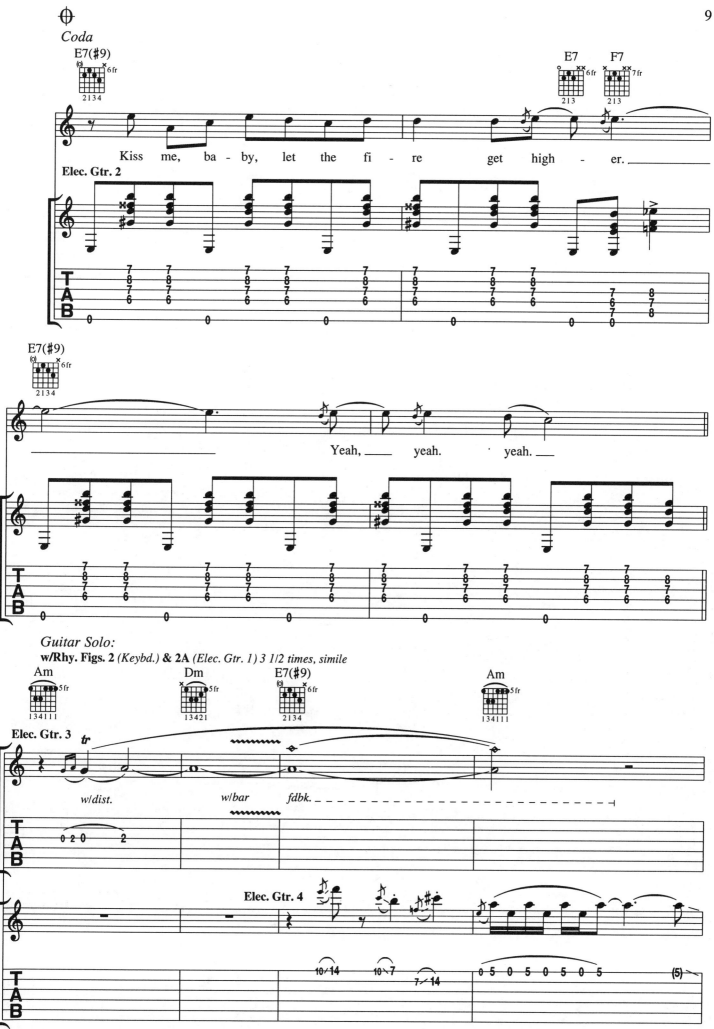

AIM FOR ME

Words and Music by
SUGAR RAY

14

Aim for Me – 6 – 3
0345B

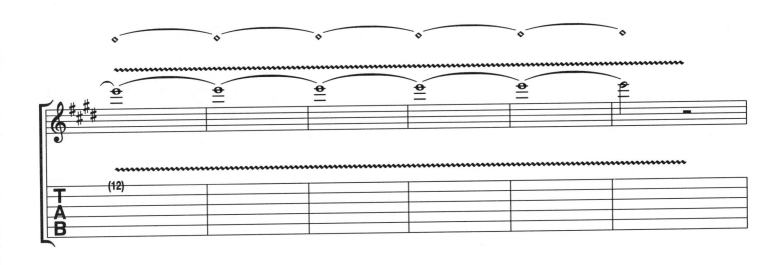

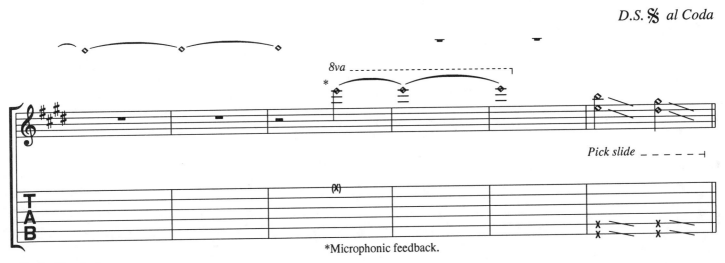

*Microphonic feedback.

Verse 2:
They'll try to count you out, but you got to count yourself in.
There's no time to throw it all away.
Not I'm saying that I'm right, seen the trouble that we've been in.
Didn't ask for nothing along the way.
(To Pre-chorus 2:)

Pre-chorus 2:
When it's said and done and you got us on the run,
That's okay, we'll never come undone.
Some people change and your life will rearrange,
Even when you're so far from home.
(To Chorus:)

BURNING DOG
(a/k/a (Don't Pet a) BURNIN' DOG)

Words and Music by
SUGAR RAY

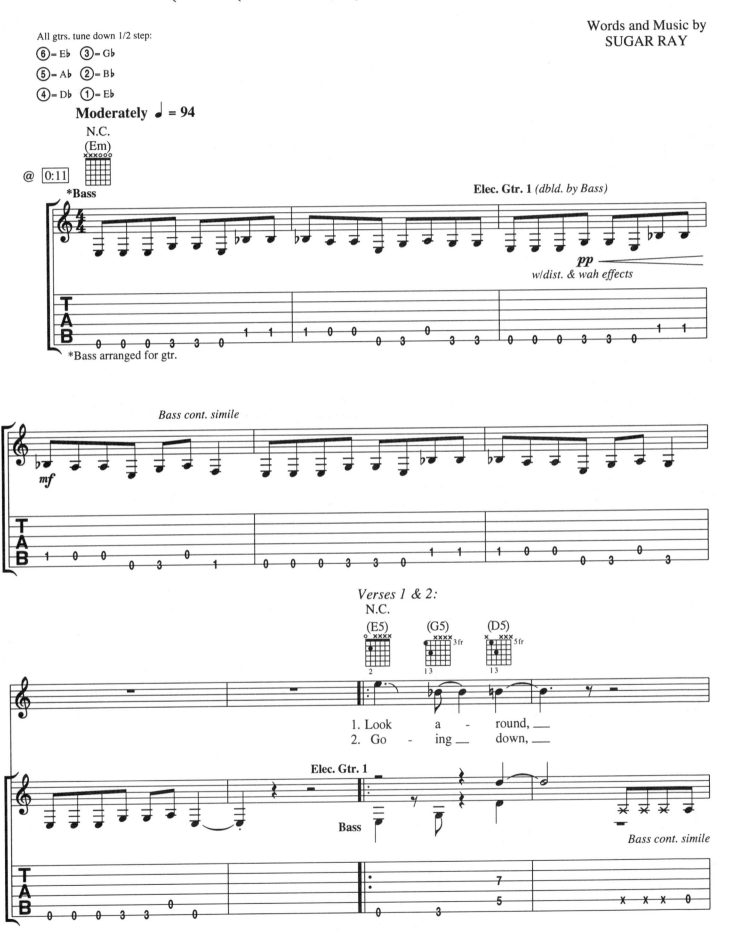

20

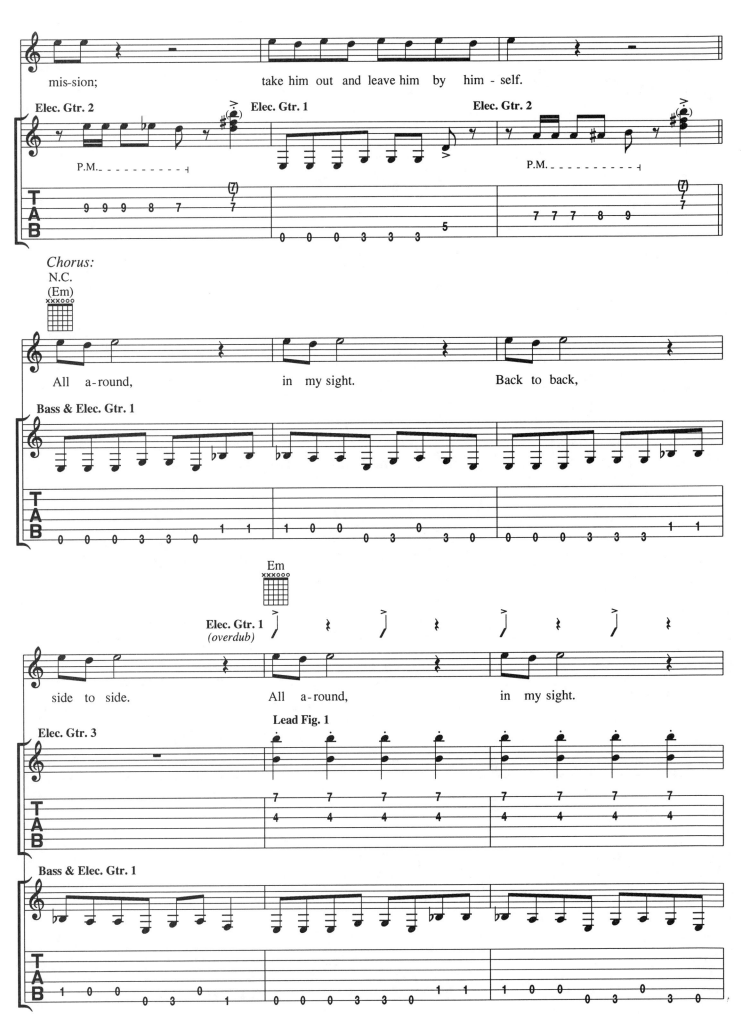

Back to back,   side to side.   Yeah!

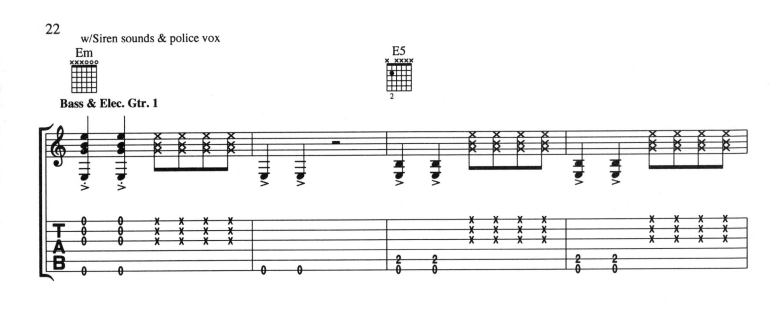

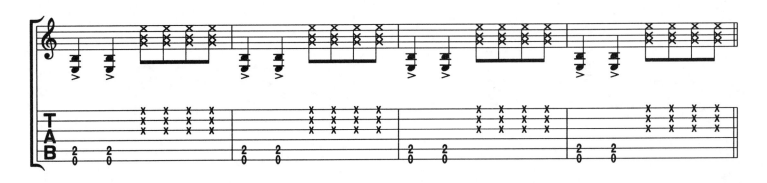

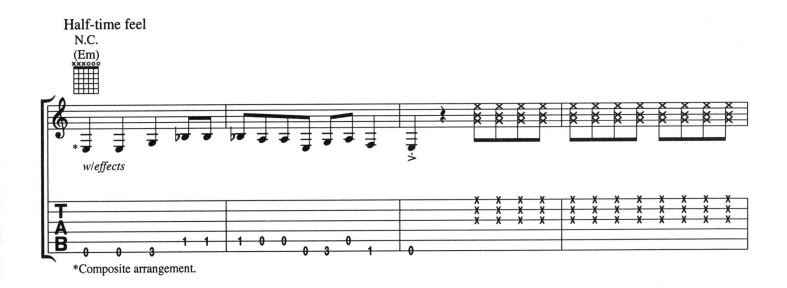

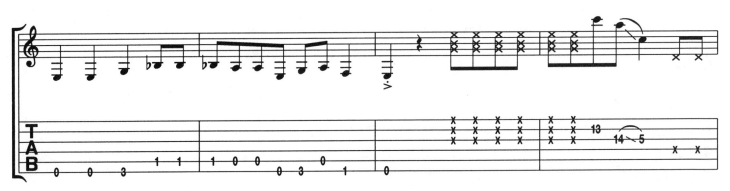

24

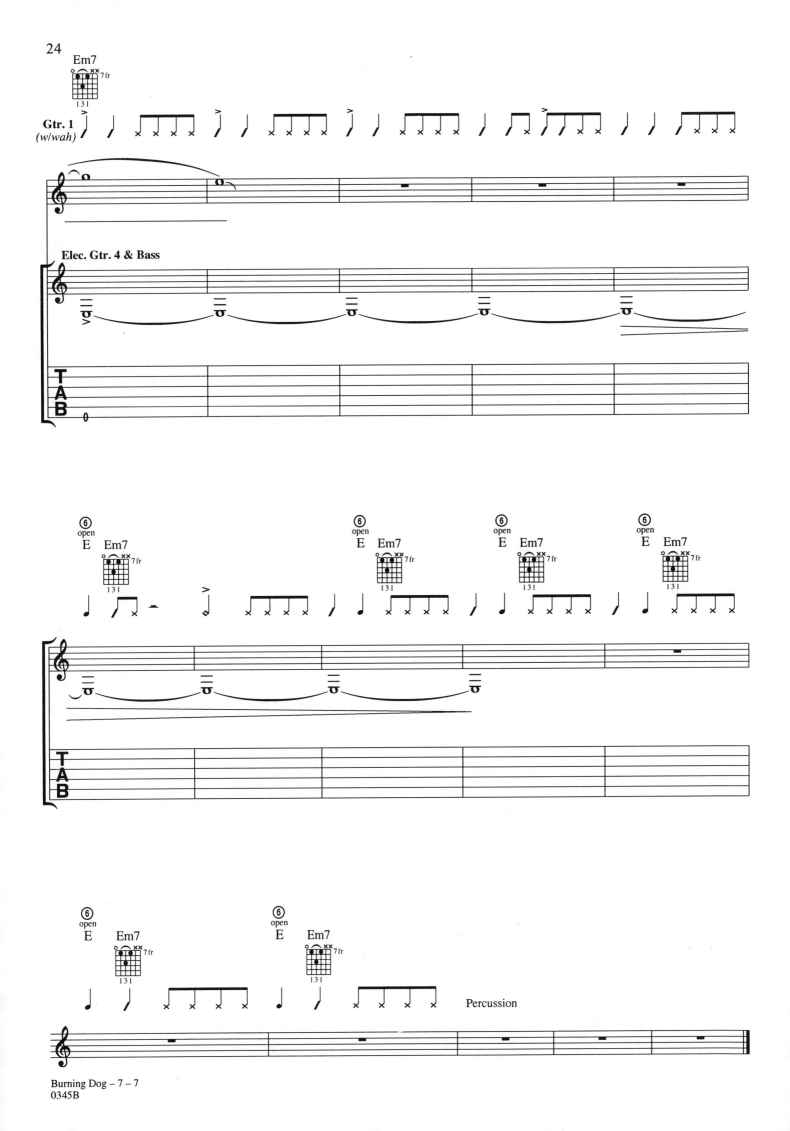

EVERY MORNING

Words and Music by
SUGAR RAY, DAVID KAHNE, RICHARD BEAN,
PABLO TELLEZ and ABEL ZARATE

All gtrs. tune down 1/2 step:
⑥ = Eb ③ = Gb
⑤ = Ab ② = Bb
④ = Db ① = Eb

Moderately ♩ = 110

N.C.

Intro:

Acous. Gtr. 1

Riff A

end Riff A

mf

T A B

w/Riff A *(Acous. Gtr. 1)*

A   E   D   E   A   E   D

Acous. Gtr. 2

mf

Cont. rhy. simile

Verse 1:

Acous. Gtr. 1 out

E   A   E   D   E

Ev - 'ry morn - ing there's a ha - lo hang - ing from the cor - ner

A   E   D   E   A   E   D

of my girl-friend's four-post bed. ___ I know it's not mine, but I'll

Acous. Gtr. 2 out

E   A   E   D   E

see if I can use it for the week-end or a one-night stand. ___ Could-n't

Every Morning – 7 – 1
0345B

30

Verse 4:

Ev - 'ry morn-ing there's a ha - lo hang-ing from the cor - ner of my girl-friend's four-post bed.__

I know it's not mine, but I'll see if I can use it for the

week - end or a one-night stand.__ (Shut the door, ba - by, don't say a word.)

EVEN THOUGH

Words and Music by
SUGAR RAY

Even Though – 6 – 1
0345B

Chorus:

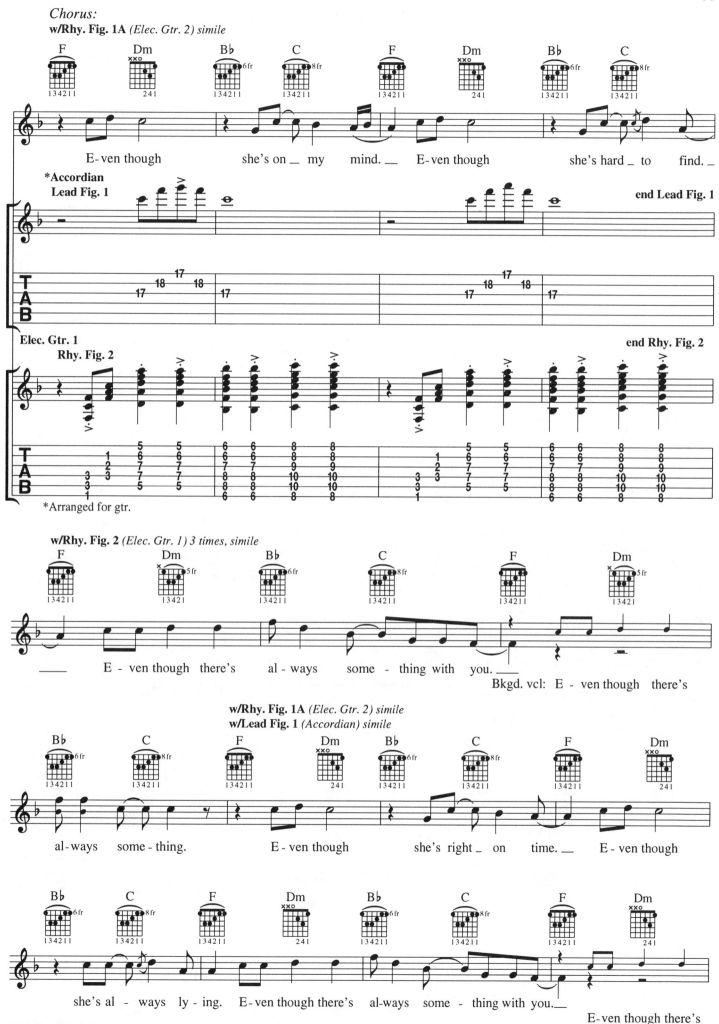

34

al - ways   some - thing.

*Two gtrs. arranged for one gtr.

Bridge:

Oh, I know ___ we don't ___ talk a - bout ___ it.

I know _ that that's   true.   Oh, I know _ we don't _

Even Though – 6 – 3
0345B

To Coda

talk a - bout _ it. { I'm so scared that I'm los-ing you.
I'm so lone - ly a - way from you.

Chorus:
w/Lead Fig. 1 *(Accordian) simile*
w/Rhy. Fig. 1A *(Elec. Gtr. 2) simile*
w/Rhy. Fig. 2 *(Elec. Gtr. 1) 2 1/2 times, simile*

E - ven though she just _ stopped try - ing. E - ven though

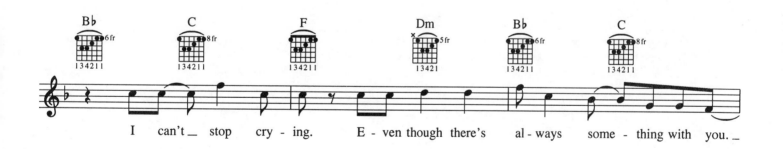

I can't _ stop cry - ing. E - ven though there's al - ways some - thing with you. _

w/Rhy. Fig. 1A *(Elec. Gtr. 1) simile*

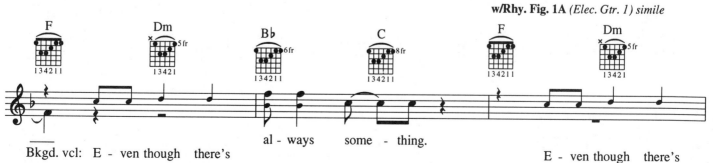

Bkgd. vcl: E - ven though there's   al - ways   some - thing.   E - ven though there's

36

*Two gtrs. arranged for one gtr.

e - ven though there's al - ways some - thing with you. _

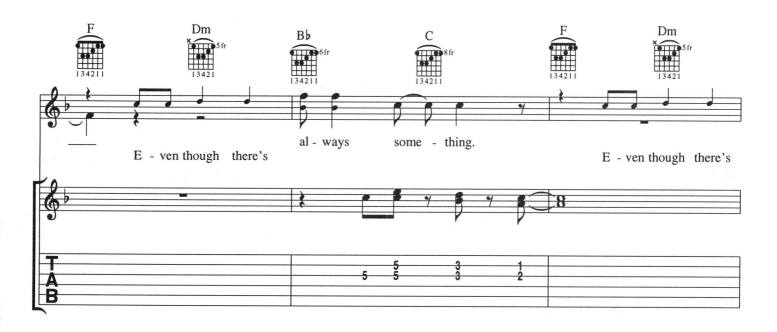

E - ven though there's al - ways some - thing. E - ven though there's

Elec. Gtr. 1

al - ways some - thing with you. _

poco rit.

FALLS APART

Words and Music by
SUGAR RAY and DAVID KAHNE

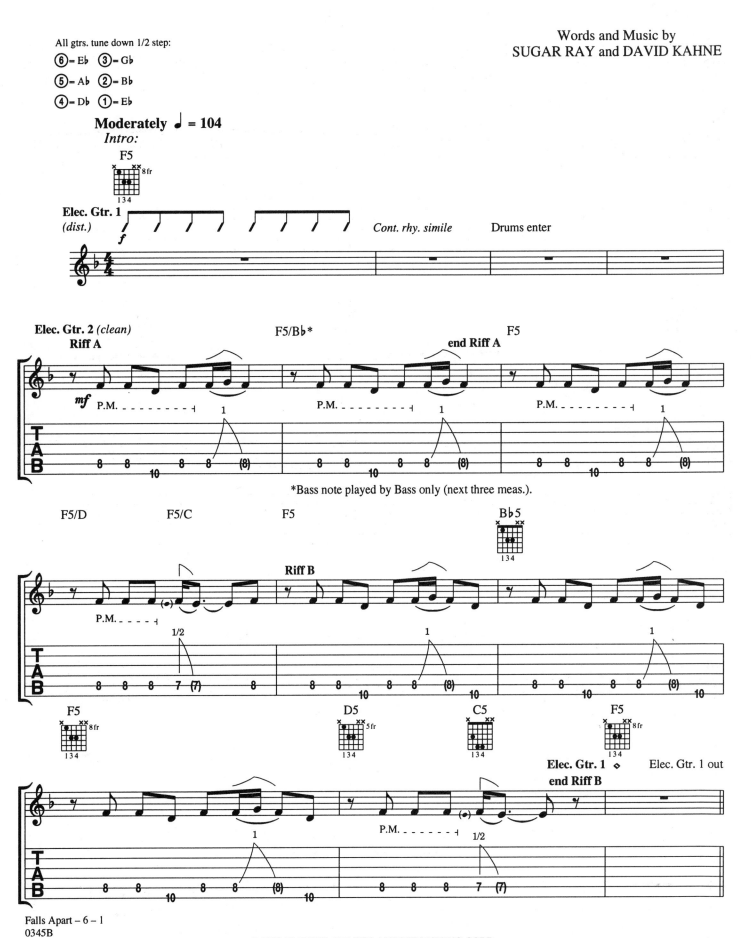

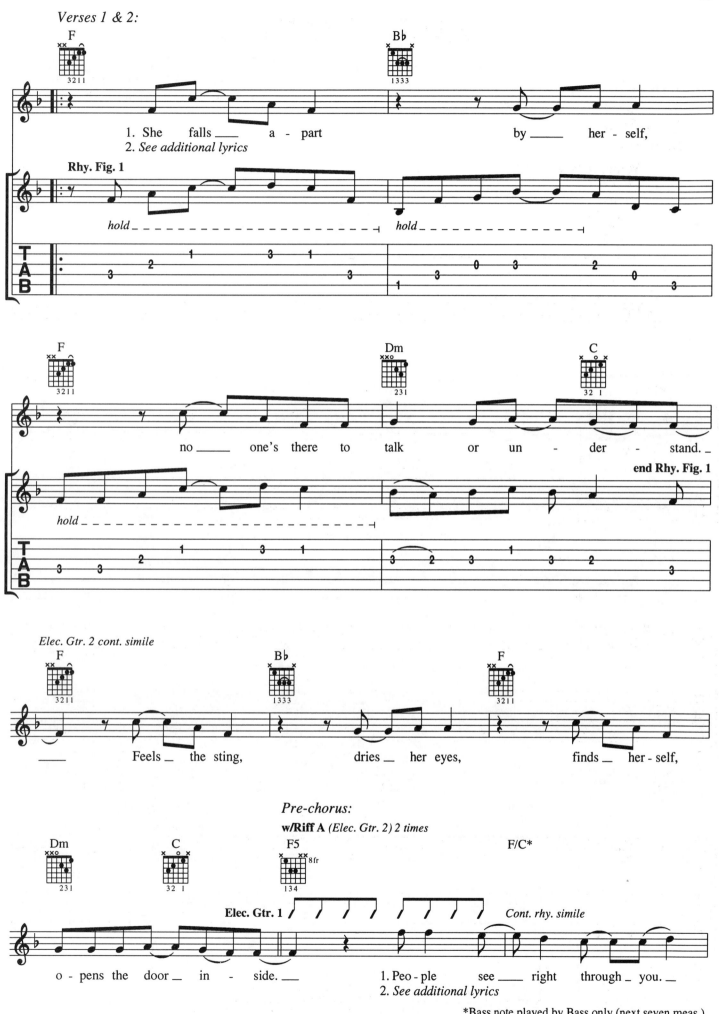

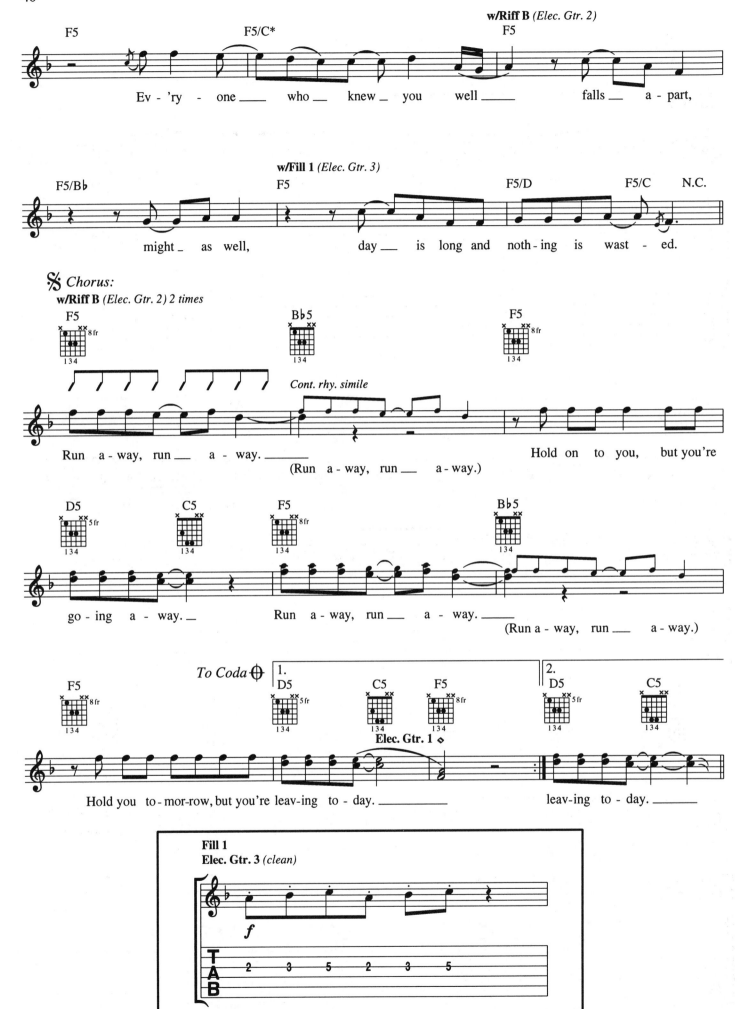

Bridge:

42

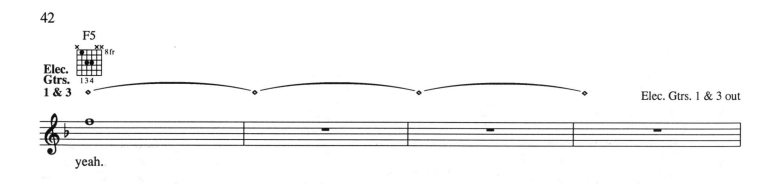

yeah.

Verse 3:
w/Rhy. Fig. 1 *(Elec. Gtr. 2)*

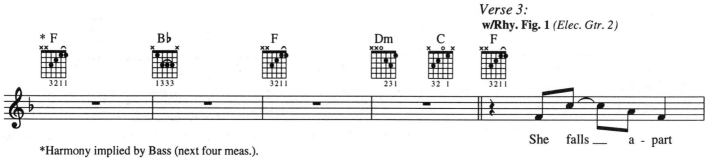

Harmony implied by Bass (next four meas.).

She falls __ a - part

no __ one there,   hold __ her hand, it seems to dis - ap - pear. __

D.S. 𝄋 *al Coda*

Elec. Gtr. 1

__ Falls __ a-part,   might __ as well,   day __ is long and noth-ing is wast-ed. __

Elec. Gtr. 2

hold   hold   hold

Falls Apart – 6 – 5
0345B

*Bass note played by Bass only.

Coda

w/**Riff B** *(Elec. Gtr. 2)*

leav - ing to - day. _____ Run a - way, run ___

___ a - way.   Hold on to you,   but you're go - ing a - way. _ But you're

leav - ing to - day, ___   but you're leav - ing to - day. _____

Outro:

Elec. Gtr. 2 out   Elec. Gtr. 1 out   Drums only   *Repeat and fade*

Verse 2:
You walk along by yourself.
There's no sound, nothing's changing.
They've gone away, left you there.
Emptiness, there's nothing you can share.
(To Pre-chorus 2:)

Pre-chorus 2:
All those words that hurt you, more than you would let it show.
It comes apart by itself, always will and everything's wasted.
(To Chorus:)

GLORY

Words and Music by
SUGAR RAY

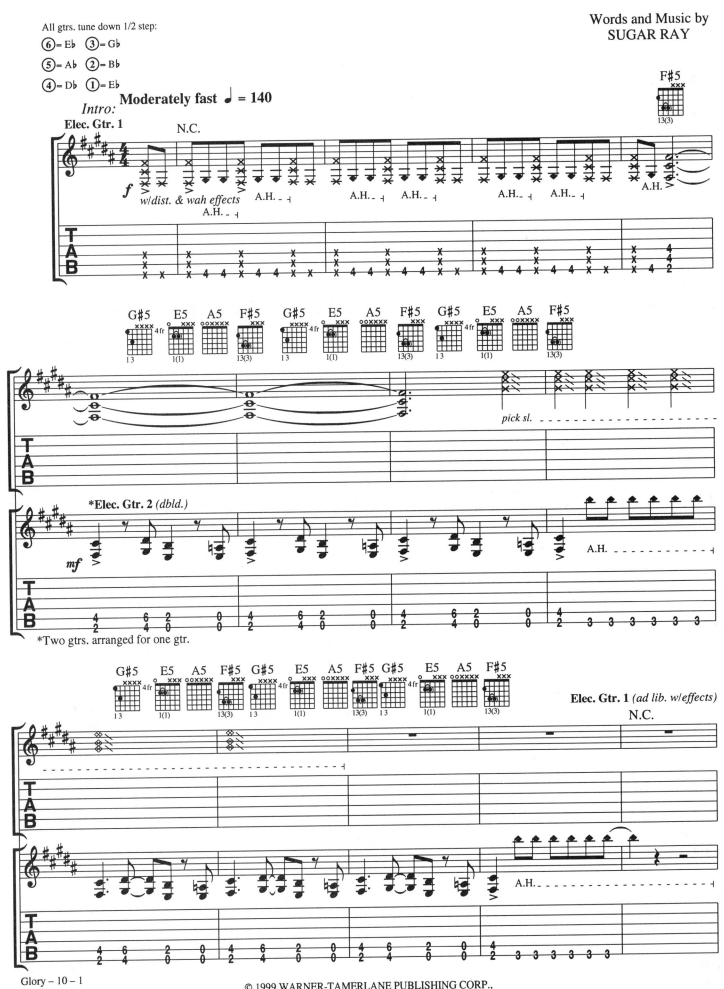

Verses 1 & 2:

1. It's good to see __ you here a - gain. __
2. Ev - 'ry-bod-y's gon - na find me out. __

Thought you al - most died. __
I'm go-ing down this time.

You nev - er win, __ well,
Ev - 'ry - bod - y's gon - na

lis - ten in,
know a - bout

you bare - ly had to try. _____
the mess you left be - hind. _____

*Chords in parentheses implied by Bass.

Glory – 10 – 2
0345B

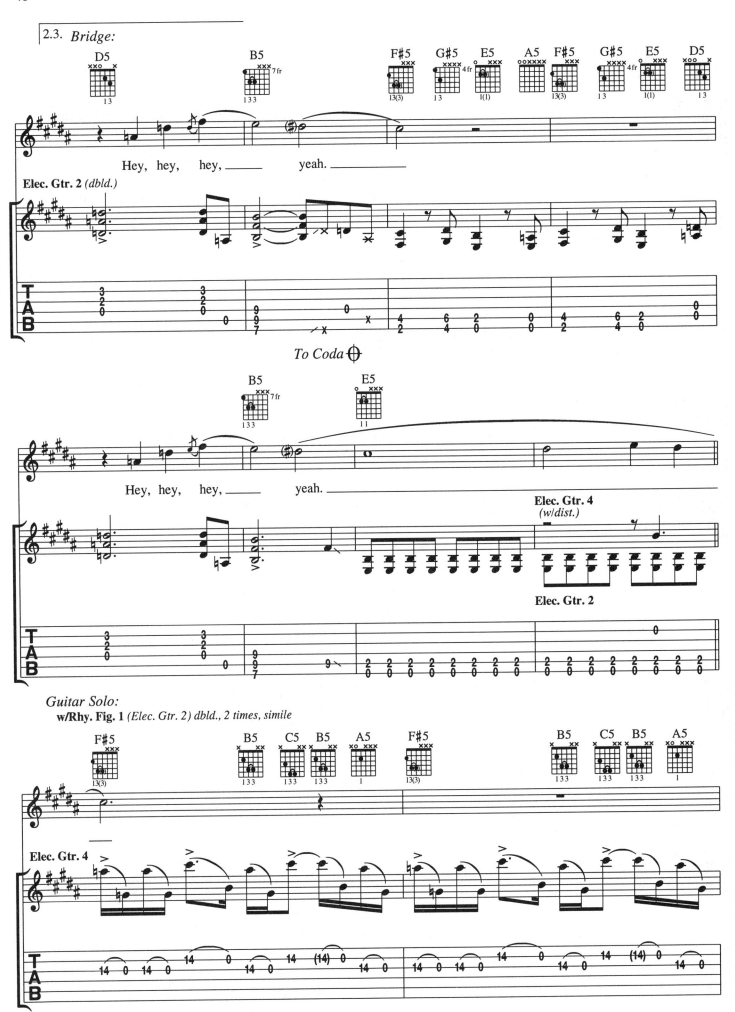

49

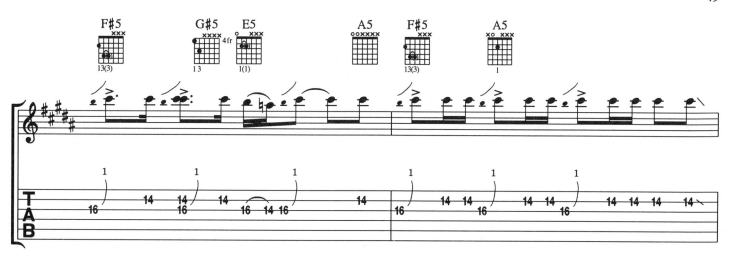

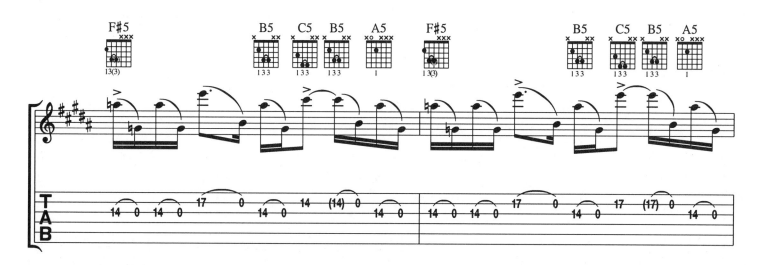

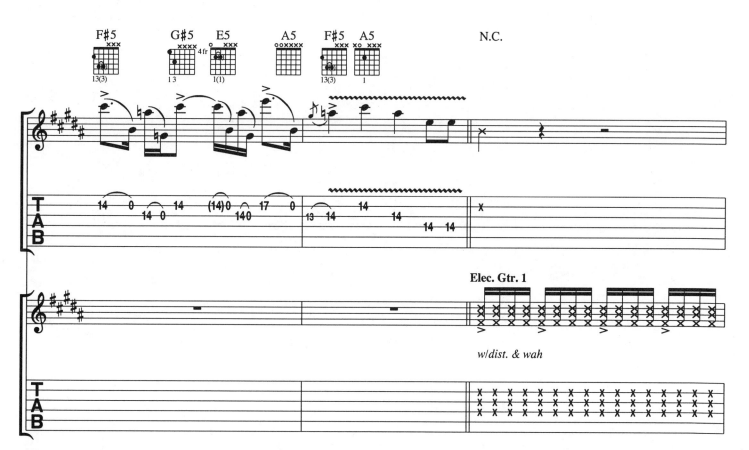

Glory – 10 – 6
0345B

50

Elec. Gtr. 1

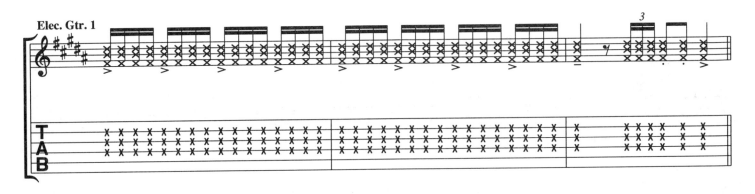

Verse 3:

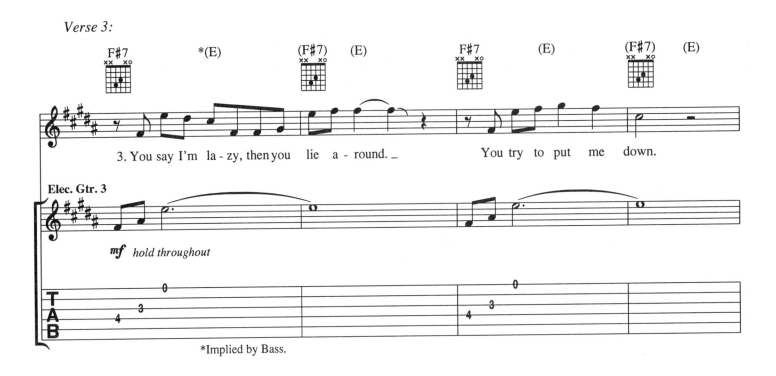

3. You say I'm la - zy, then you lie a - round. ___ You try to put me down.

Elec. Gtr. 3

mf hold throughout

*Implied by Bass.

Elec. Gtr. 3 tacet

N.C.

I know you're cra - zy when I see ___ you spin your head a - round. ___

Elec. Gtr. 1

w/dist. & wah

Glory – 10 – 7
0345B

Pre-chorus:

John - ny fall - ing from the sky. ___

Please tell me, lie af - ter lies. ___

D.S. %. al Coda

Elec. Gtr. 3

Elec. Gtr. 1

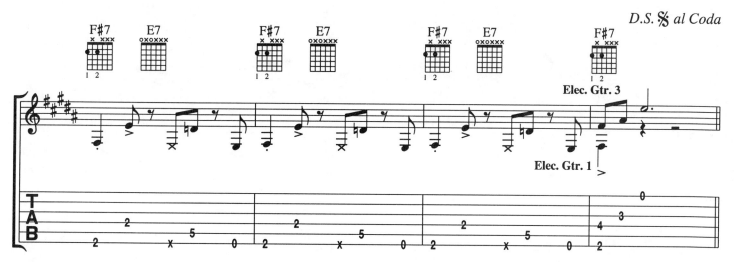

52

LIVE & DIRECT

Words and Music by
SUGAR RAY, DAVID KAHNE
and LAWRENCE PARKER (a/k/a "KRS ONE")

All gtrs. tune down 1/2 step:

⑥ = E♭ ③ = G♭
⑤ = A♭ ② = B♭
④ = D♭ ① = E♭

Moderately ♩ = 72

Intro:

Chord symbols reflect overall tonality (throughout).

Fill 1
Acous. Gtr. 2

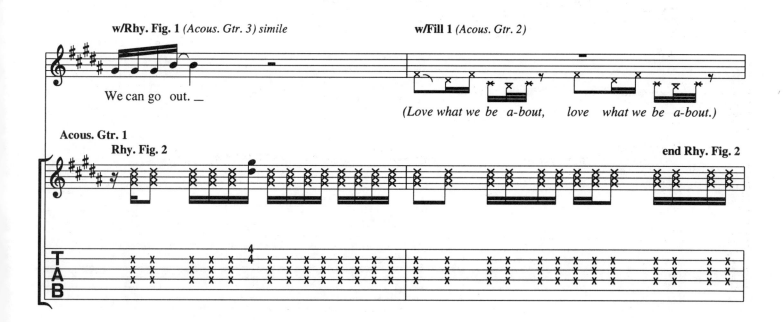

N.C.

F#7
131211

We can go out. _

(Love what we be a-bout, love what we be a-bout.)

Acous. Gtr. 1

Elec. Gtr. 1

Verse:
w/Rhy. Fig. 1 *(Acous. Gtr. 3) 4 times, simile*
w/Rhy. Fig. 2 *(Acous. Gtr. 1) 4 times, simile*

w/Fill 2 *(Acous. Gtr. 2)*

G#m
134111

G#5   A5
4fr   5fr
134   134

1. We can go out __ on the week - end __ 'cause the week - end is free.
2. *See additional lyrics*

Elec. Gtr. 1

f P.M.

G#m
134111

G#5   A5   G#5
4fr   5fr   4fr
134   134   134

We can go off of the deep end __ if you're think - ing of me. __

mf

f P.M.

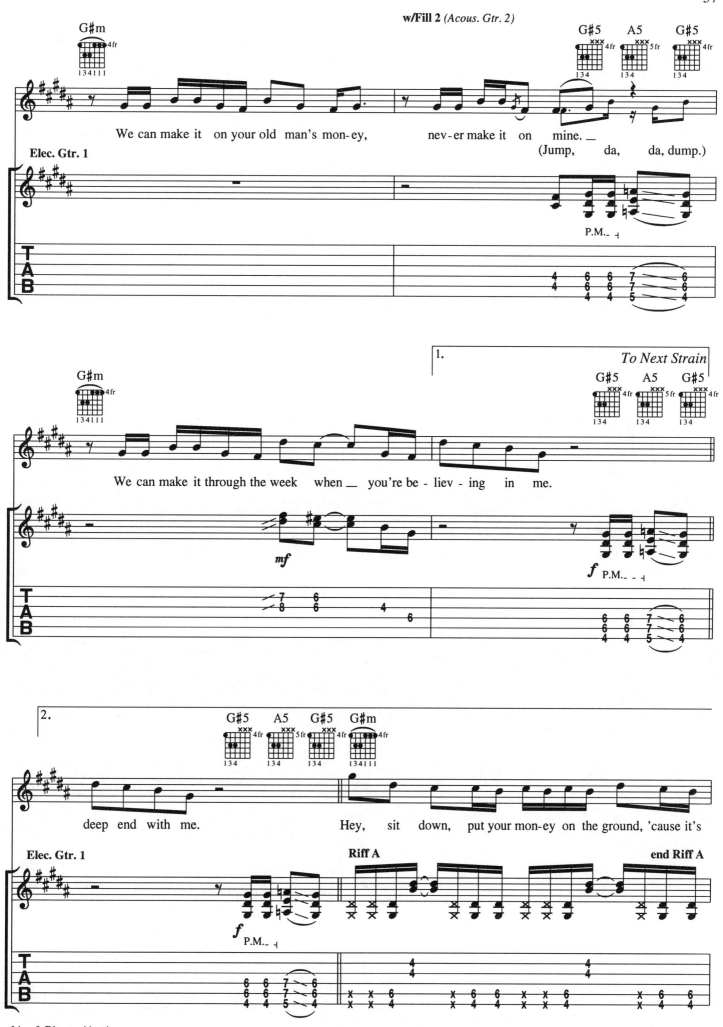

58

gon-na be a trag - e - dy. __

Hey, sit down, put your mon-ey on the ground, 'cause it's

Chorus:
Acous. Gtrs. 1 & 3 out
F#7

gon-na be a trag - e - dy. __

You're the one that said to me,

Elec. Gtr. 1

Elec. Gtr. 2

mf
w/tremolo effect

you're the one that said to me that we don't __ re - gret an - y - more. __

(What a - bout, 'bout, 'bout, what a - bout, 'bout, 'bout, what a - bout, 'bout, 'bout?)

(Love what we be a-bout, love what we be a-bout.)

It's gon-na be a trag-e-dy. ___

(Love what we be a-bout, love what we be a-bout.)

Outro:

w/Rhy. Fig. 1 *(Acous. Gtr. 3) 5 times, simile*
w/Rhy. Fig. 2 *(Acous. Gtr. 1) 5 times, simile*
w/Various ad lib. gtr. and vocals throughout

w/Fill 2 *(Acous. Gtr. 3)*

Jump, dump, dah, dump, da, da, da, da, da, dump. Jump, dump, dah, dump, da, da, da, dump, da, dump.

*Elec. Gtrs. 1 & 2

P.M. throughout

*Two gtrs. arranged for one.

Jump, dump, dah, dump, da, da, da, dump, da, dump. Jump, dump, da, dump, da, da, da, dump. *Not e,*
(We can go out __ on the week - end.)

64

Verse 2:
We can get out on the weekend, everybody can see.
We can drive off the deep end, if you depend on me.
We can make it, you can make it, never make it on time.
Lose your mind on the weekend, off the deep end with me.
Hey, sit down, put your money on the ground, 'cause it's gonna be a tragedy.
Hey, sit down, put your money on the ground, 'cause it's gonna be a tragedy.
(To Chorus:)

NEW DIRECTION
(Track 1)

Words and Music by
SUGAR RAY

66

Verse:

w/Rhy. Fig. 1 *(Elec. Gtr. 1) 2 times*

w/Rhy. Fig. 2 *(Elec. Gtr. 2) 3 times*

(Spoken:) Be nice to your sister,   talk to your   grandmother,

paint her a picture.   Don't play ball in the house,

Outro:

Play 3 times

don't run with scissors,   be nice to cops.

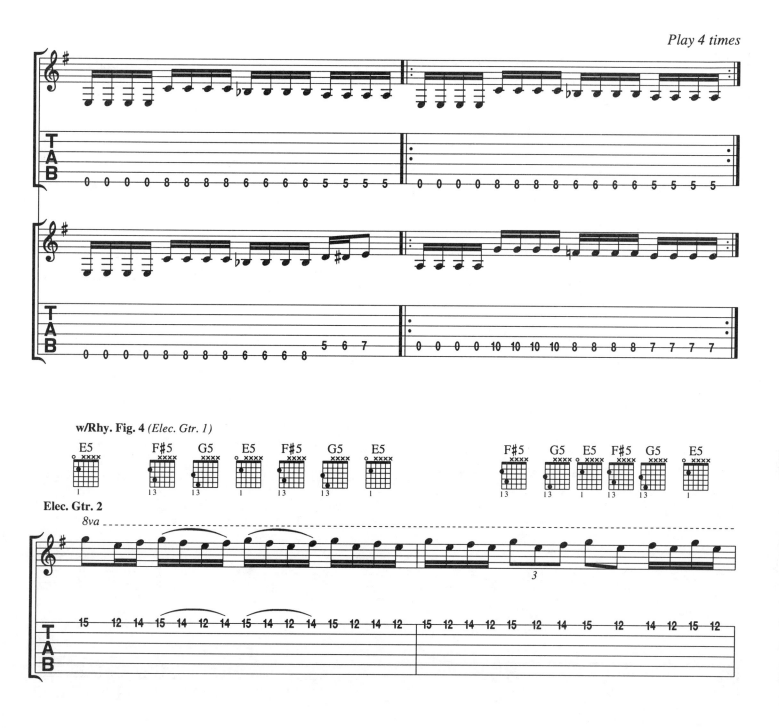

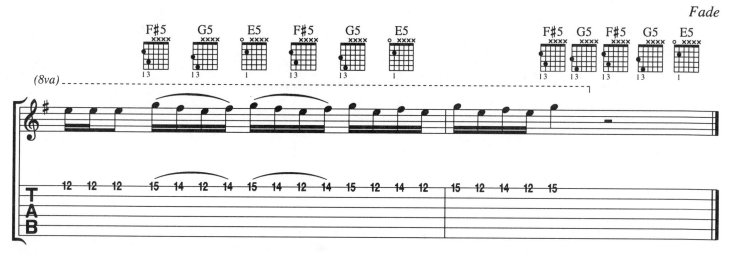

68

NEW DIRECTION
(Track 13)

Words and Music by
SUGAR RAY

69

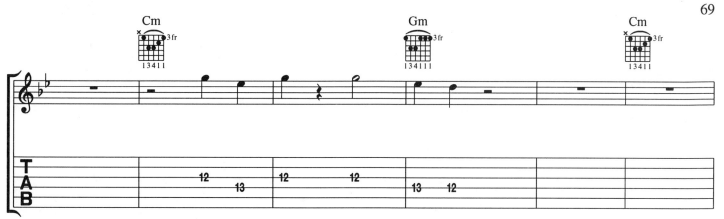

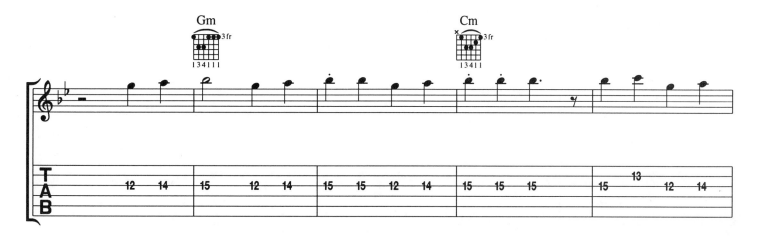

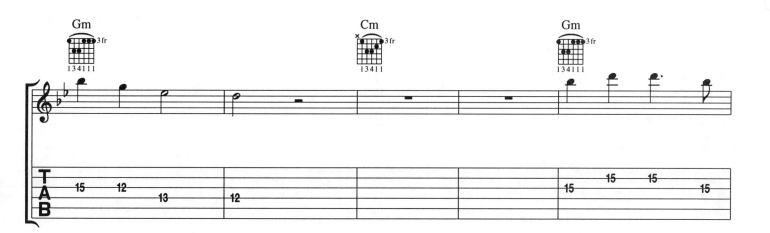

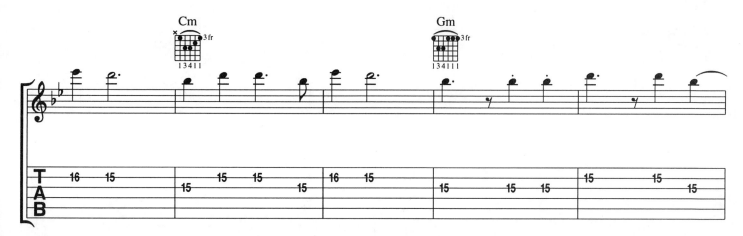

New Direction – 4 – 2
0345B

70

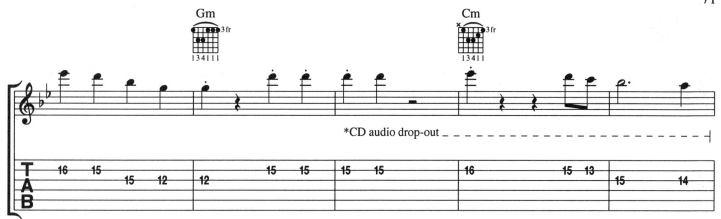

*CD audio drop-out _

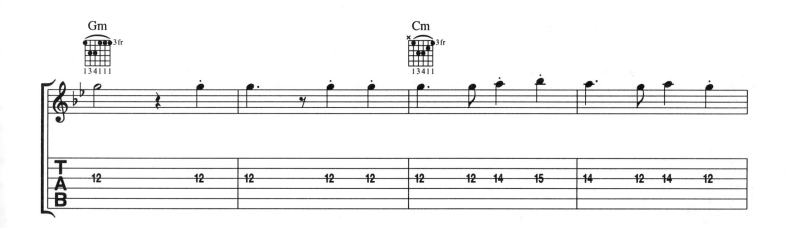

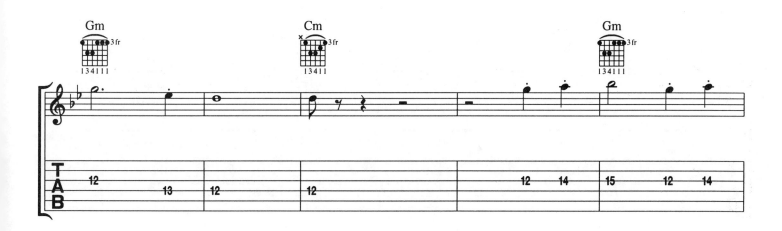

Begin fade   *Fade*

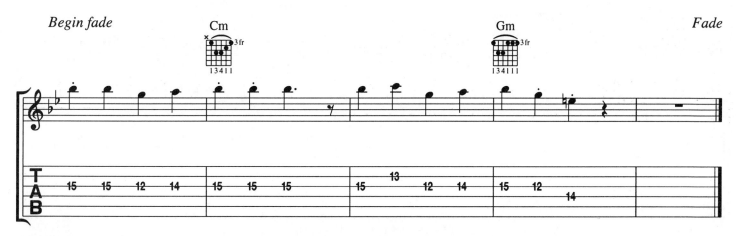

New Direction – 4 – 4
0345B

ODE TO THE LONELY HEARTED

Words and Music by
SUGAR RAY and NICK SOPKOVICH

All gtrs. tune down 1/2 step:

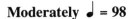

Moderately ♩ = 98

Intro:

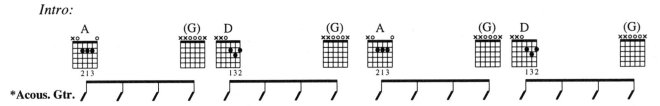

*Composite arrangement of Acous. gtr. and Piano.

Verse 1:

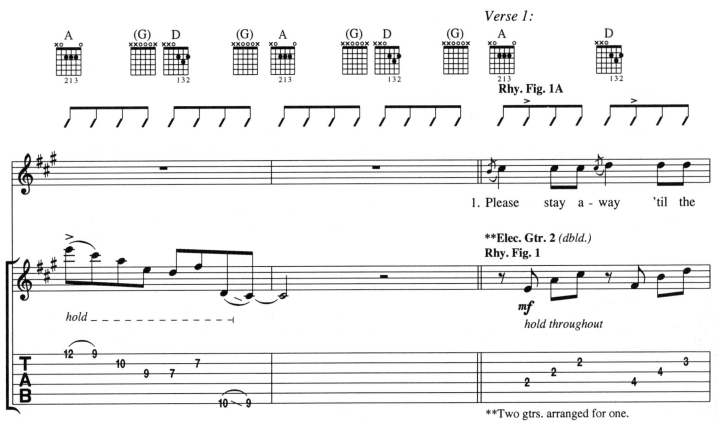

1. Please stay a-way 'til the

**Two gtrs. arranged for one.

Ode to the Lonely Hearted – 6 – 1
0345B

end Rhy. Fig. 1A

end of the night _ when noth-ing's _ on _ the run. _

end Rhy. Fig. 1

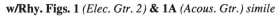

w/Rhy. Figs. 1 *(Elec. Gtr. 2)* & 1A *(Acous. Gtr.)* simile

Please stay a-way 'til I ___ can't fight _ the rea-son _ and _ the thought. _

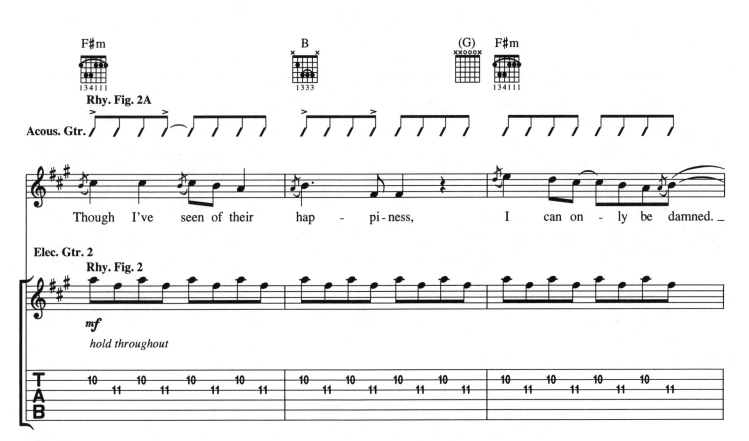

Rhy. Fig. 2A

Acous. Gtr.

Though I've seen of their hap-pi-ness, I can on-ly be damned. _

Elec. Gtr. 2

Rhy. Fig. 2

mf

hold throughout

74

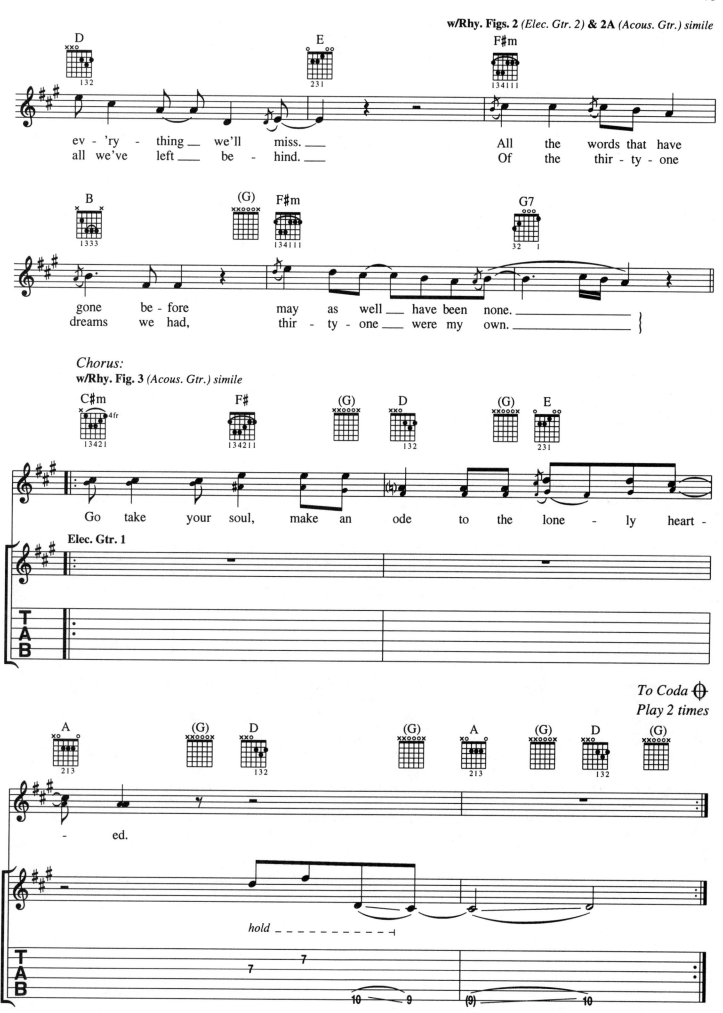

76

Bridge:

Ode to the Lonely Hearted – 6 – 5
0345B

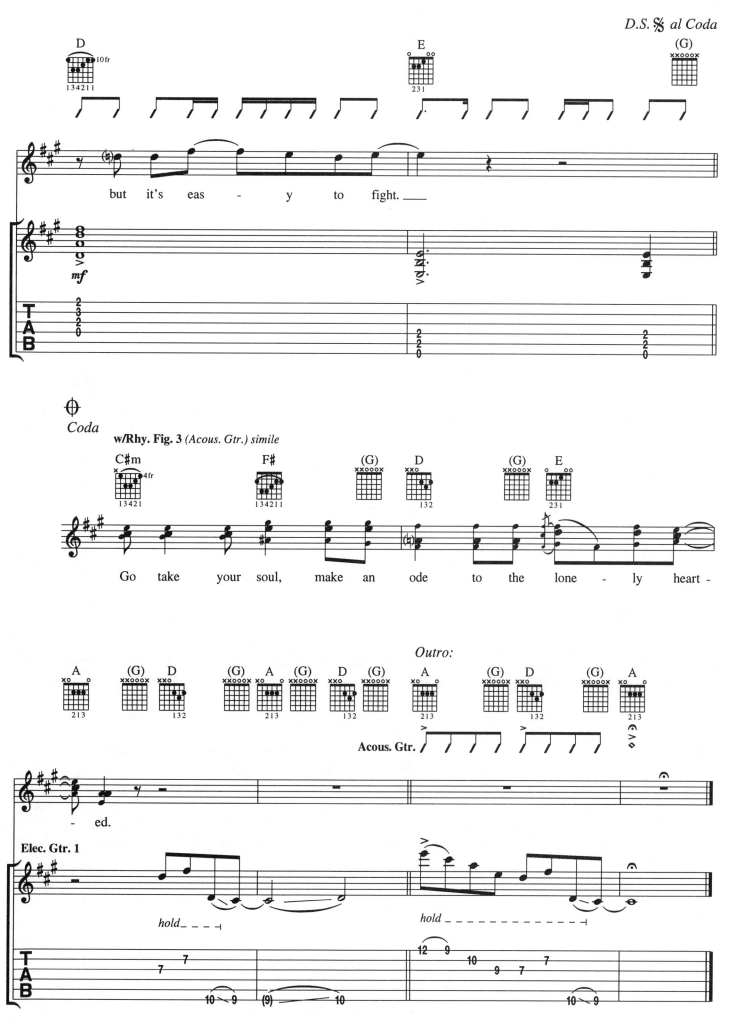

PERSONAL SPACE INVADER

Words and Music by
SUGAR RAY and DAVID KAHNE

All gtrs. tune down 1/2 step:
⑥ = E♭   ③ = G♭
⑤ = A♭   ② = B♭
④ = D♭   ① = E♭

Fast rock ♩ = 168

Play 3 times

Intro:

Play 4 times

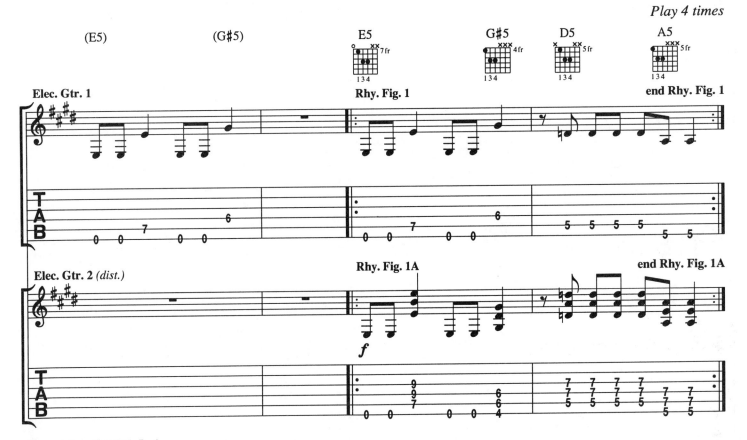

Personal Space Invader – 7 – 1
0345B

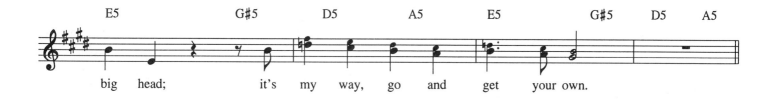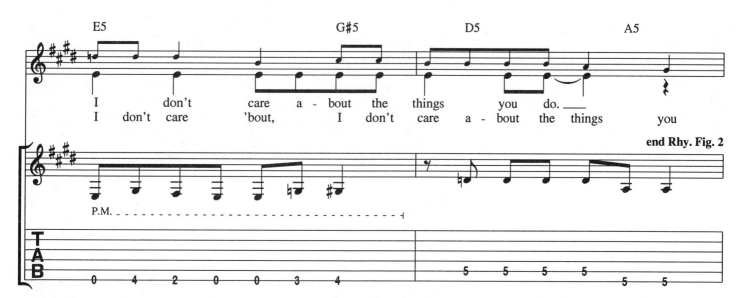

Personal Space Invader – 7 – 2
0345B

80

*Vocals first time only.

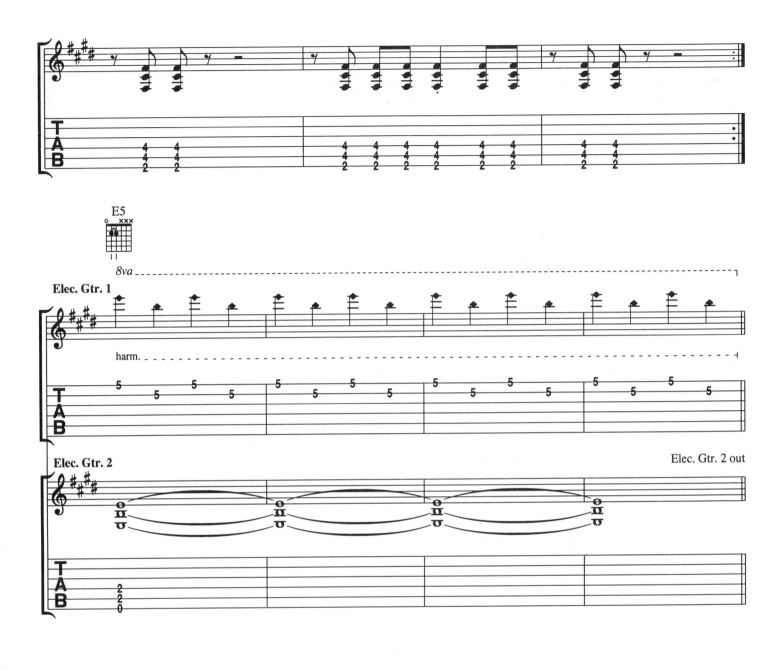

Verse 4:
w/Rhy. Fig. 1 *(Elec. Gtr. 1) 4 times*

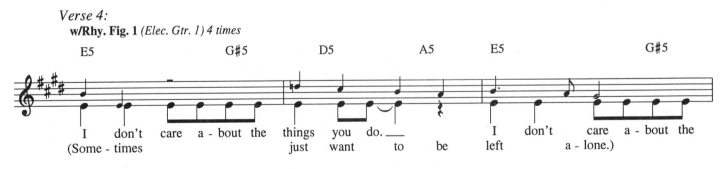

I don't care a - bout the things you do.___ I don't care a - bout the
(Some - times just want to be left a - lone.)

things you do. ___ I don't care a - bout the things you do. ___ and
(Move your big head; it's my way, go and

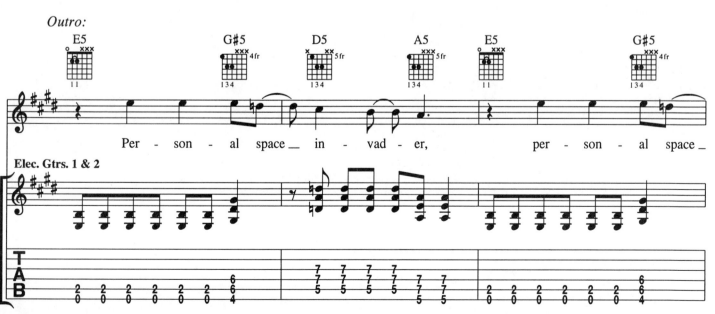

Personal Space Invader – 7 – 6
0345B

Verse 2:
Want more, impossible to satiate.
Got the high score, forgot to put the letter eight.
(To Pre-chorus 2:)

Pre-chorus 2:
I don't know about the things you do.
I don't know about the things you do.
I don't know about the things you know about
The things I know about the things you do.
(To Chorus:)

Verse 3:
Now that I take a vow we made
Or the illegal pictures on the net.
Ooh, remember how we taught you well
And that you played right into gate to hell?
(To Pre-chorus 3:)

Pre-chorus 3:
I don't know about the things you do.
I don't know about the things you do.
I don't know about the things you do.
I don't care about . . .
(To Chorus:)

Someday

Words and Music by
SUGAR RAY and DAVID KAHNE

1. Some-day, when my life has passed me by, __ I'll lay a-round and
2. *See additional lyrics*

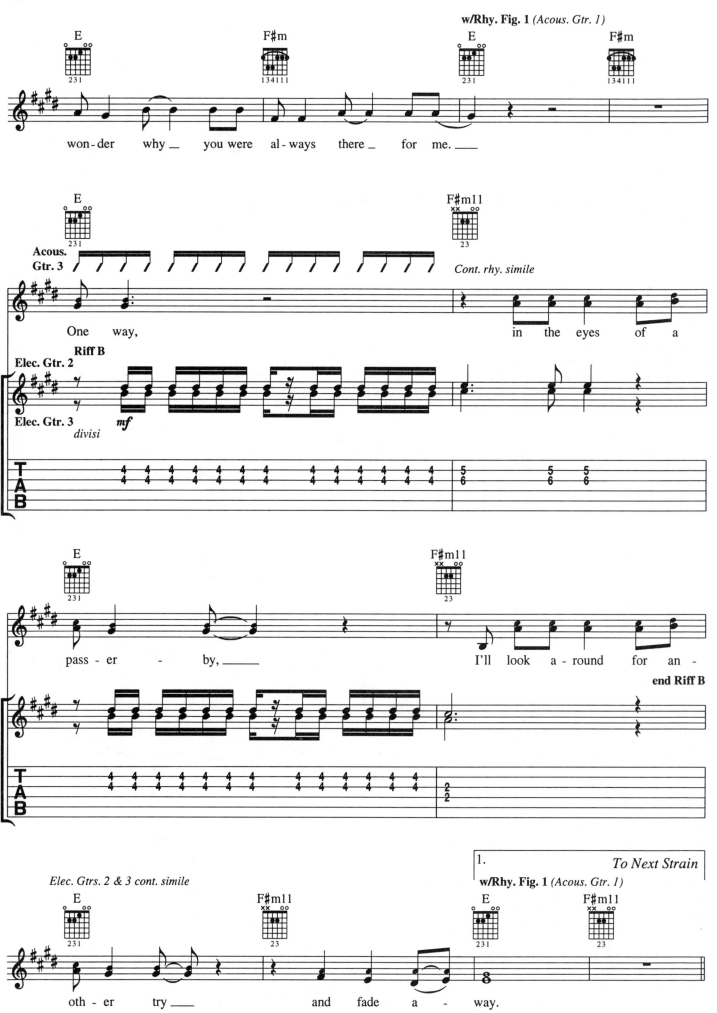

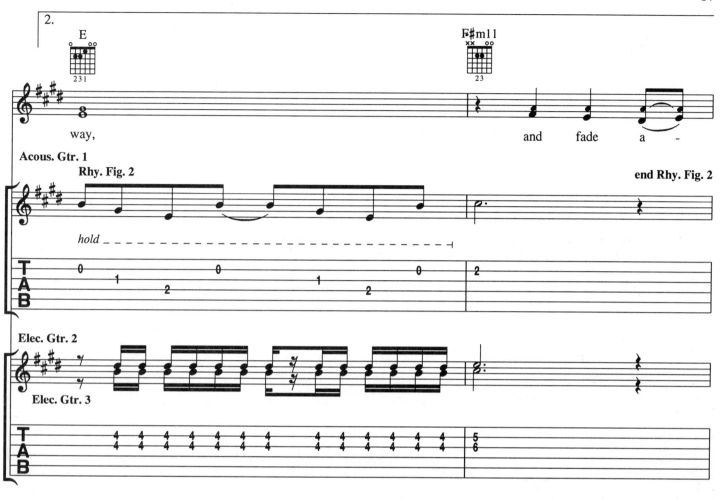

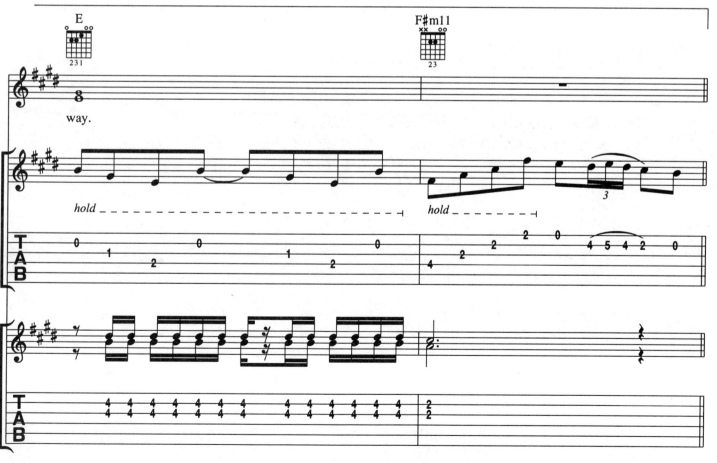

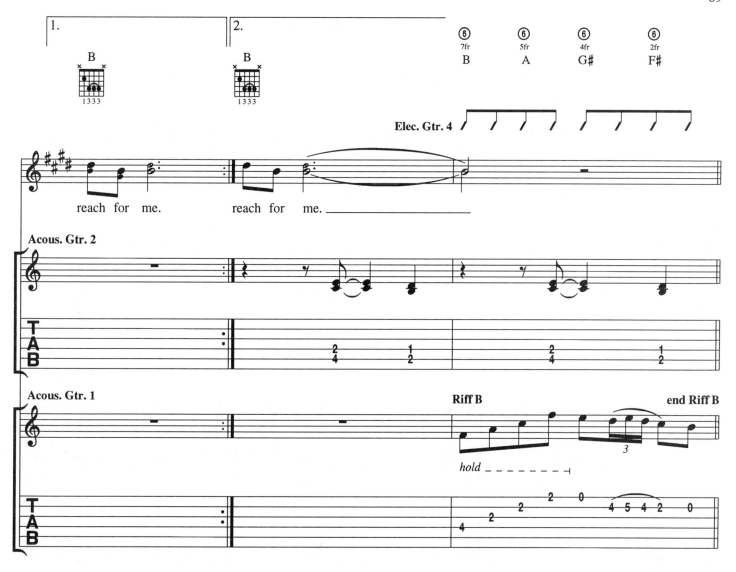

reach for me.   reach for me.

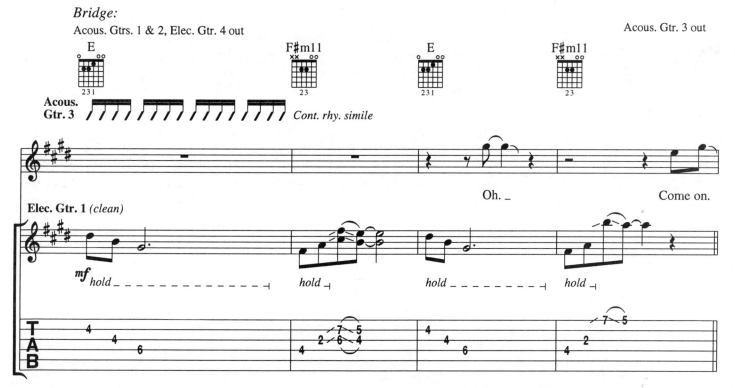

Oh. _   Come on.